A Girl's Guide to

yoga

Over 30 poses to practice anywhere

Jeanne Finestone

Illustrations by
Shelly Meridith Delice

SCHOLASTIC INC.

New York Toronto London Auckland Sydney
Mexico City New Delhi Hong Kong Buenos Aires

yoga

ISBN-13: 978-0-439-89662-7
ISBN-10: 0-439-89662-2

12 11 10 9 8 7 6 5 4 3 2 1   6 7 8 9 10 11/0

Printed in the U.S.A.   40

First Scholastic printing, October 2006

While the advice and information in this book is believed to be accurate and the step-by-step instructions have been devised to avoid strain or injury, the author and the publisher disclaim any liability from any injury that may result from the use, proper or improper, of any exercise or advice contained in this book.

Parents and teachers should be aware of a child's physical condition and health and match exercises, positions, and advice to the appropriate skill level and abilities of the child.

Please consult a professional health care provider for information and advice on the suitability of any exercise program.

CREDITS

Creative Directors
Tanya Napier and Hallie Warshaw

Writer
Jeanne Finestone

Graphic Designers
Tanya Napier and Domini Dragoone

Illustrator
Shelly Meridith Delice

Editor
Erin Conley

Production Artist
Domini Dragoone

Created and produced by Orange Avenue Publishing
San Francisco, CA

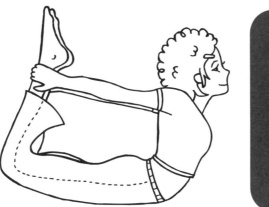

A Girl's Guide to

yoga

Table of Contents

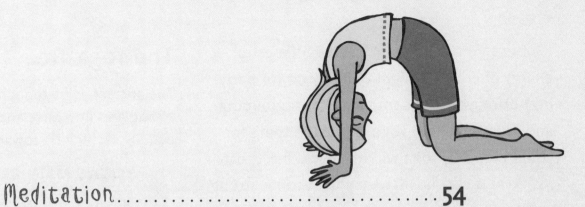

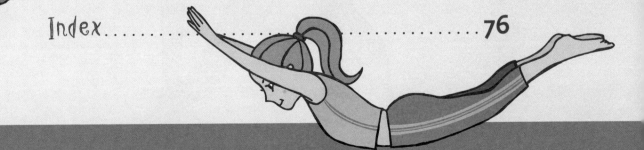

What's Yoga All About?

Is stress getting to you? Need a little extra energy after a late night of studying (or partying) or maybe just some time for regrouping and relaxing? Then yoga is just the thing for you. Practicing yoga will make you feel great—inside and out. It will help you become strong and limber no matter what your body type or ability level. It will also help you develop a positive, healthy attitude and a peaceful mind, carrying over into all aspects of your life!

The word yoga comes from an ancient Sanskrit word that means "union." The goal of yoga is to unite the body, mind, and spirit—to allow the yogi (that's you!) to live life in harmony with herself and the world around her.

The Yoga Tree

The ancient yogis thought of yoga as a tree with a strong and firm base and different branches (or paths) reaching up toward the sky.

YOGA'S MAIN BRANCHES

KARMA   This is the path of action. Karma yogis practice good deeds unattached to personal desires or results. If you do volunteer work (or other selfless good deeds), you're a Karma yogi.

BHAKTI   This is the path of love and devotion to God, the Divine. Nuns, monks, or any others who dedicate their life to the Divine are Bhakti yogis.

RAJA A Raja yogi strives to control the mind and senses to achieve *samadhi*, where she is one with the Divine.

JAPA Japa is part of Raja yoga. It includes the continuous repetition of a *mantra* (sound vibration), or positive affirmation, which helps to focus the mind in meditation.

JNANA This is the path of wisdom and learning. It stresses the study of spiritual texts to learn the great spiritual secrets of the Universe.

Everybody's Doing It

Yoga may be the world's oldest discipline, but it's pretty hip and trendy these days. Over 30 million people from all over the world—and even lots of celebrities—are hooked!

Superstar Yogis

Sheryl Crow

Sting

Halle Berry

Madonna

Penelope Cruz

David Duchovny

Lisa Leslie

Phil Jackson

Orlando "El Duque" Hernandez

Annika Sorenstam

Grant Hill

The Chicago Cubs

Evander Holyfield

Cindy Crawford

The Miami Dolphins

Hatha Yoga

Hatha is the most popular branch of yoga—and the one most people mean when they say they practice yoga. It's also the one you'll be learning as you work with this book. Hatha combines the practice of specific poses, focused relaxation, breathing exercises, and meditation. Regular practice of Hatha yoga helps you in lots of different ways.

Benefits of Hatha

Builds strength and coordination.

Increases flexibility.

Promotes a healthy body.

Focuses and calms your mind.

Makes you feel good about yourself and the world around you.

Yoga for Every Body (and Mind)

Just as there are many branches of yoga, there are many different styles of Hatha. There are even styles within the styles. You'll want to take your time to discover the one that works best for you.

HATHA STYLES

IYENGAR   This form of Hatha focuses on very detailed physical aspects of yoga's many poses. Iyengar often uses props like blocks, belts, and chairs. It's the most popular style of Hatha yoga practiced in the United States.

VINYASA   In Vinyasa yoga, the poses flow into one another. When combined with rhythmic breathing, it gives your mind and body a super intense workout.

KUNDALINI   Kundalini combines breathing, chanting, and mantras with postures. It wakes up the *kundalini*, which is a serpent-like energy stored at the base of the spine, and draws it up through the seven *chakras* (or energy centers of the body).

BIKRAM   This is a fixed series of Hatha poses practiced in a super hot, humid room. Be prepared to get sweaty!

INTEGRAL   Integral yoga encourages the integration of all of yoga's teachings into your everyday life. It's based on the philosophy that yoga's goal is to have an "easeful body, a peaceful mind, and a useful life."

No matter which type of yoga you practice, a complete yoga session usually starts with the poses, moves to deep relaxation, then to breathing practices, and closes with meditation. As you explore yoga and become more comfortable in your own personal practice, try to move from the physical to the mental level and to incorporate a deeper, subtler awareness.

A Very Brief History of a Very Old Tradition

Yoga is over 5,000 years old and is the oldest ongoing system of personal development in the world. It is believed that around 200 B.C.E. a wise man named Patanjali gathered the core principles into 196 threads (or sutras) of yogic philosophy. Because of this work, The Yoga Sutras, Patanjali has come to be considered the father of yoga. However, it was Swami Vivekananda who is recognized as having introduced yoga to the West at the Chicago Parliament of Religions in 1893.

Is yoga for me?

One of the many great things about yoga is that it's not something you need to be good at. It's something that you do because it's good for you. You don't need to be thin, athletic, flexible, or able to sit for long hours on a bed of nails. You don't need fancy clothes or equipment—and you don't need to pay lots of money for lessons. You can do it all by yourself, with friends, or in a class. All you really need is the desire to be your very best, to relax, and to enjoy yourself.

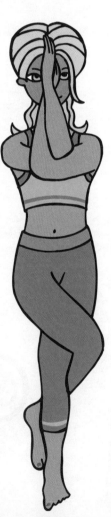

Yoga Speak

Before you hit the yoga mat, there are a few terms you should know. You'll find a full list of tongue-twisting terms in the glossary, but these will get you started!

SANSKRIT   The new words you've learned so far are in Sanskrit. Sanskrit is the basis for the different Indian dialects, and it is the language of yoga. Some of the words are tricky to pronounce, but learning them will make it easier for you to explore and expand your practice.

ASANA   A yoga posture is called an *asana*, which means steady, comfortable pose. Each of the asanas offers a number of health benefits, and practicing Hatha yoga regularly strengthens and tones your entire body.

PRANA   Ancient cultures recognized that all life—from the smallest ant to the entire universe—is sustained by an unseen, ever-present energy. In yoga, this energy is called *prana* or life force. It is the same thing as the Asian *chi* or *qi*.

AHIMSA   *Ahimsa* is a powerful concept in yoga. It's often understood to mean nonviolence, but its literal translation is "not causing pain." The ancient yogis meant this in the broadest sense. They believed that even the simple act of speaking a cruel word can be hurtful to yourself and others.

NAMASTE   *Namaste* means "the divine in me honors the divine in you." It is the traditional yogic and Hindu greeting. It is also the name of the position where you hold your hands together in front of your chest as if in prayer.

OPENING UP THE HEART   Opening up the heart is not really a technical yoga term. But it's a good concept to remember when you practice. When you're instructed to "open up the heart" or "expand the chest," you're supposed to expand your chest area physically. However, you are also supposed to be opening yourself up to all the possibilities the world has to offer. A person with an open heart walks tall and strong and is happy to greet the world.

Yoga is a complex, wonderful, ancient practice. Open up to it—learn and enjoy. Your body and mind will thank you!

Preparing to Practice

Just like you need to stretch before you play sports, it's good to prepare for yoga.

Things to Have

CLOTHING   Comfortable, loose-fitting clothing is best. Also, have a sweatshirt and socks nearby for Yogic Sleep.

PROPS   You really don't need to buy any special equipment. Many yogis like to practice with a "sticky mat" to keep from slipping, but a bath towel will do just as well. Also, you might want to grab a cushion (or additional bath towel) to help you adapt certain poses to your individual needs.

SPACE   Yoga is best practiced in a nice, quiet space. If you can, dim the lights so it's not too bright. Some people like to play music while practicing; others find it distracting. If you do play tunes, be sure to choose a type of music that is soothing and relaxing.

Things to Avoid

FOOD   Try not to eat for two hours before practicing. Also, to maximize digestive benefits, wait at least an hour after you practice before you chow down. A small drink of warm water before you start can be very beneficial.

Things to Think About

BREATHING   It may sound silly, but in yoga, concentrating on your breath is very important. It can really make a difference in how you feel and enhance the benefits you get from the poses. Always breathe through your nose, slowly and deeply. Unless otherwise instructed, keep your belly relaxed so you can expand it as you inhale and contract it as you exhale.

INSTRUCTION   You don't need to practice in a group or with a teacher, but there are lots of advantages in doing so. A teacher can help solve problems, answer questions, and correct your posture for maximum results.

No Wounded Yogis!

Anyone can practice yoga, and everyone who does will benefit from it. But before you begin, check with your doctor—especially if you have any kind of health condition. Yoga is known to promote good health, but everybody has different needs and challenges. So play it safe! Read the "Tips from the Yogis" and "When to Be Careful" in each section. Also be sure to let your yoga teacher (if you have one) know of any problems so he or she can help you adapt poses to suit your needs.

One of the only real "don'ts" in Hatha is, "Don't go beyond what your body can do." Challenging yourself is good, but only go as far as you can without strain. Hold the poses for as long as they feel comfortable. Come into the poses gradually and with control. Try to be aware of any tightness in your body. If you're feeling stress or strain, ease up or slowly (and carefully) come out of the pose.

There are no hard-and-fast rules about how long to hold each pose, but there are some general guidelines on what to work up to as a new yogi. (Don't worry too much about it being exact!)

- Standing and Balancing poses: 30 seconds

- Backward-Bending poses: 15–30 seconds (ideally twice per pose)

- Forward-Bending poses: 30–90 seconds

- Twists: 30 seconds

- Yogic Sleep: Up to you—whatever feels good!

Yoga is not a competition. Like so many things in life, what comes easily one day may be tough the next. Remember, every day is different. Just notice the changes and work with them. And one last thing ... HAVE FUN!

How to Sit

- Cross-legged on the floor with (or without) a small cushion under your buttocks.

- On your knees with your buttocks resting on your heels. This is Hero pose.

- On a solid, straight-backed chair.

The most important thing is to be comfortable and steady—so just experiment with what works best for you.

Body Check

- Keep your back straight (but not stiff).
- Relax your abdomen.
- Relax your shoulders down and away from your ears.
- Your chin should be parallel to the floor.
- Gently close your eyes and lips.

Take Stock

Once you're comfortable, focus on your breath. Breathe naturally, without forcing or changing your breathing. Begin to observe the effects of your inhalations and exhalations. Notice how your abdomen naturally expands and contracts, how your shoulders rise and fall, and how your body shifts and changes with each breath.

Mind Over Matter

Don't be surprised if you find your mind wandering. You might start thinking about tomorrow's test or Saturday's party. That's okay. When you catch yourself drifting, just gently bring your mind back to your breathing. Feel yourself relax.

Ready to Practice

You are now ready to begin your practice. In the next section, you will be introduced to a series of poses that, when put together, can offer you a complete pose practice.

❋ Eye Movements ❋
Netra Vyayamam

Beginning a session with *Netra Vyayamam* is a wonderful way to help focus and calm the mind. Like all asanas, this exercise can have many positive physical benefits. Try it after working on your computer, watching TV, or some intense reading. You'll be amazed at the relief!

Benefits

- Strengthens the eye muscles.
- Relieves eyestrain.
- Improves eyesight.

When to Be Careful

- Don't do eye exercises if you have any problems with your eyes.
- Be sure to remove eyeglasses and hard contact lenses.

1 Start with your eyes closed. Imagine the face of a clock.

2 Gently open your eyes and look up to twelve o'clock.

3 Move your eyes slowly in a clockwise direction, touching each and every number on the clock, first one, then two, then three, and so forth. Continue at your own pace for as many cycles as are comfortable.

4 Finish by looking up to twelve o'clock. Gently center and close your eyes. Inhale deeply and exhale with control.

5 Practice the above in a counter clockwise direction.

Relaxing Your Eyes

1 Keeping your eyes closed, rub your palms together briskly to build up heat.

2 Cup your palms over your eyes, inhale the warmth from your palms, and exhale any tension.

3 When you feel the warmth subside, use your fingertips to massage your head, face, neck, and shoulders.

4 Return your hands to your lap (or knees) and enjoy the effects of the eye exercises.

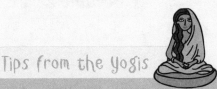

Tips from the Yogis

- Move only your eyes slowly and steadily.
- If you're having trouble, use your finger to guide your eyes around the circle.
- Gaze as far to the edge of your vision as possible without straining.
- Soften your vision (almost like you're not really looking at anything).
- Don't forget to breathe!

❀ Sun Salutation ❀
Surya Namaskaram

Sun Salutation is a *vinyasa*, a series of 12 positions that flow gracefully into each other. Its Sanskrit name has a pretty impressive translation—"I bow to you oh beautiful light."

It's good to practice Sun Salutation 2 to 4 times at the beginning of each yoga session. Move slowly during the first round to help limber up the body. Be sure to concentrate on how your body feels in each position, and become aware of places where you may be especially loose or tight.

Benefits

- Wakes up the entire body.
- Prepares you for asana practice (and other athletics).
- Works all the joints.
- Develops muscle strength and stamina.
- Helps cool down the body after strenuous exercise.

Position 1

✿ Mountain ✿ Tadasana

Mountain pose opens and closes Sun Salutation, but it's also the foundation for many of the standing and balancing poses. This pose gets its name because you stand straight and tall like a majestic mountain.

Benefits

- Improves your posture.
- Steadies your mind.
- Strengthens your back and stomach muscles.

1 Stand with your feet together or up to hip-width apart.

2 Distribute your weight evenly throughout your feet, from your toes to your heels and from the inner to the outer edges.

3 Straighten your knees without locking them. Your hips should be directly over your ankles.

4 Your spine should feel very long as you relax the muscles of your back, buttocks, and inner thighs. Tuck your tailbone in slightly.

5 Open your chest by bringing your shoulders back and away from your ears.

6 Stretch the top of your head toward the sky, and keep your chin parallel to the floor.

7 Place your hands by your side or in Prayer position (Namaste).

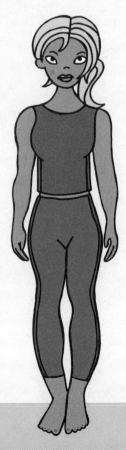

Position 2

1 Lock your thumbs together. Stretch your arms out in front of you, and then lift them up alongside your ears.

2 Gently arch your back from just below the shoulder blades. Feel the stretch at the front of your body as you elongate your back muscles.

Inhale.

Position 3

1 Bend forward from your hips, keeping your back straight for as long as it's comfortable, and elongate the spine.

2 Relax and let your head and arms dangle toward the floor.

3 Feel the stretch in your hamstrings, calves, and lower back. If your fingers touch your toes, great. If not, just hang comfortably. If your lower back feels tight, bend your knees.

Exhale.

Position 4

1 Bend your knees. Place your fingertips alongside your toes.

2 Stretch your left foot far back. Bring your left knee to the floor.

3 Stretch your chest forward and up.

4 Check to see that the lower half of your right leg is perpendicular to the floor with your right knee over your right ankle.

5 Feel the stretch in your thighs as you relax your pelvis toward the floor.

Inhale.

Position 5

❀ Downward Dog ❀
Adho Mukha Svanasana

In Sanskrit, *svana* means "dog" and *adho mukha* means "downward facing." Think of a dog stretching—its head and forelegs reaching toward the floor and its hind legs reaching up toward the ceiling. Downward Dog is position 5 and 8 of *Surya Namaskaram*. Many yogis like to rest for a few deep breaths when they are in this pose.

Benefits
- Relieves tightness in the legs.
- Strengthens the arms, wrists, and chest.
- Reenergizes the body.

When to Be Careful
- Don't stay too long in Downward Dog if you have low blood pressure.

1 Keep your hands and left foot as they were when you finished position 4. Bring your right foot back to align with your left, keeping your buttocks high in the air and your legs straight.

2 Your hands should be slightly more than shoulder-width apart, and your head should be between your arms. Your feet should be about hip-width apart.

3 Stretch your heels toward the floor. (Don't worry if they don't actually touch the floor). If your lower back is sore, bend your knees a bit.

4 Place your palms flat on the floor. Hold your arms straight. (From the side, you should look like an upside-down "V.")

5 Feel the stretch in your hamstrings, calves, arms, and through the spine. You are now in Downward Dog!

Exhale.

Position 6

1 Keep your hands and feet as they were when you finished position 5.

2 Slowly bring your knees, then your chest, and then your chin to the floor.

3 Keep your pelvis raised about an inch or two (3 to 5 cm) off the floor.

Exhale.

Position 7

1 With your hands and feet still as they were from when you finished position 6, move your upper body forward and bring your pelvis to the floor.

2 Gently stretch your head, neck, and chest forward and then lift them off the floor without putting pressure on your hands.

3 Be careful not to crunch up your neck.

Inhale.

Position 8

1 While putting pressure on your hands, push yourself back up into an inverted "V" (or Downward Dog), just like in position 5.

Exhale.

Position 9

1 While bending your knees, swing your left foot forward between your hands.

2 Bring your right knee to the floor. (If it's difficult to bring your foot all the way forward, bring both knees to the floor first and use your left hand to help bring your left leg forward.)

3 The lower part of your left leg should be perpendicular to the floor (with your left knee over your left ankle).

Inhale.

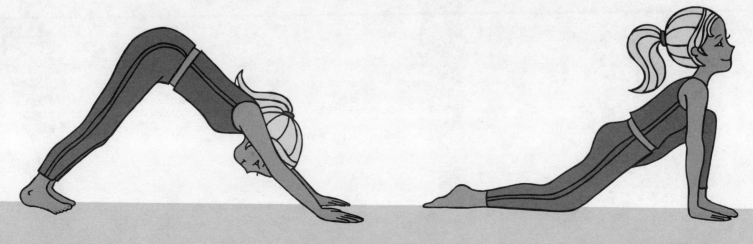

Position 10

1 Bring your right foot forward to meet your left.

2 Hang forward.

Exhale.

Position 11

1 Lock your thumbs, and stretch your arms up alongside your ears, lifting your upper body forward and then up.

2 Keep your legs straight (or slightly bent), and stretch yourself upright.

3 Gently arch your back from the shoulders.

Inhale.

Position 12

1 Bring your arms forward, and begin to stand up straight in Mountain pose.

2 Keep your arms in front of your chest in Namaste.

3 Inhale and exhale slowly with control.

4 Lower your arms to your sides, separate your legs, and relax.

Exhale.

Breathing for Sun Salutation

Once you've mastered the sequence of Sun Salutation, you can begin to incorporate the breathing practices (noted after each instruction). Breathe slowly and rhythmically through the nose as you move through each position. Hold each position for as many breaths as is comfortable, moving into the next position with the appropriate inhalation or exhalation.

Tips from the Yogis

- You might want to stretch a little before starting Sun Salutation. (See suggestions on page 60.)
- Remember to breathe through your nose.
- Once you're comfortable with the sequence, you can practice Sun Salutation as slowly or as quickly as you like and for as many times as feels comfortable.

Standing and balancing poses are about empowerment. Mountain, Tree, Warrior, Eagle—their very names bring to mind visions of strength, power, and balance. While each pose has specific benefits, in general these poses are good for building balance, focusing the mind, and purifying the nervous system.

As you become more experienced in your practice, you may want to experiment by incorporating some of the standing poses into your Sun Salutation practice.

Tree Vrikshasana

Like the oak tree, yogis need to be grounded and firm. And like the willow, they need to move and adapt to the changes in the wind.

Benefits
- Strengthens your legs, hips, and ankles.
- Opens your hips and shoulders.
- Expands your heart.
- Builds confidence.

1 Start in Mountain pose (page 19).

2 Shift your weight to your left foot.

3 Bend your right knee and bring your right foot up along the inside of your left leg as high as is comfortable without losing your balance. Your right knee should be out to the side and your hips should face the front and be even.

4 Bring your hands together in front of your chest in Prayer position and hold for a few seconds.

5 On an inhalation, raise your arms up overhead and straighten your elbows, keeping your hands together or opening up into a "V." If you feel you may lose your balance, keep your hands in Prayer position.

6 To come out of the pose, bring your hands back to Prayer position, then release your arms and legs.

7 Inhale deeply and exhale slowly with control.

8 Practice on the reverse side.

Tips from the yogis

- Concentrate on a fixed spot on the wall in front of you to help maintain balance.
- Use your hand to help place your foot.
- If you need to, try using the wall for balance, standing with it either behind you or to the side of your bent knee.
- Start by placing the foot of your bent leg next to the ankle of the standing leg. As you build confidence in subsequent sessions, move the foot up the leg to the calf, then the knee, and eventually the inner thigh.
- Don't be surprised if one side is easier to do than the other.

Warrior II ✿ Virabhadrasana II

The yoga Warrior has strength, stamina, and a sense of being firmly grounded on her own two feet. She is both confident and determined in her quest to accomplish her goals.

Benefits

- Strengthens your calves, quadriceps, and buttocks.
- Opens your hip and shoulder joints.
- Stretches your arms.
- Tones your muscles and aids digestion.
- Increases your resolve.

When to Be Careful

- If you have back problems, practice this pose with caution. If there is any discomfort, avoid it altogether.

1 Stand in Mountain pose.

2 Spread your legs about 4–4 1/2 feet apart. Open your right foot out to a 90° angle, and bring your left foot inward to a 45° angle. Check to see that your hips are squared center.

3 Raise your arms parallel to the floor in line with your shoulders, palms facing the floor. As you extend your arms, feel your shoulders reach back and down, opening up your chest.

4 Keeping your torso upright and your left foot firmly on the floor, exhale while you bend your right knee and turn your head to look out over your right hand. Your left leg should remain straight.

5 Tuck in your buttocks so you're not leaning forward. Feel the stretch in your inner thighs.

6 Inhale back to standing.

7 Reverse the leg position and repeat on the other side. You can rest in Corpse (page 38) when you are finished.

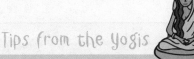

Tips from the yogis

- Make sure that your bent knee does not extend beyond your foot.
- If your knee feels stressed, loosen up or come out of the pose.
- To keep your body in line, imagine that you are standing between two walls running closely parallel to one another.
- Keep your gaze steady for balance.

When your back is strong and flexible, you can stand up to anything! Backward bending poses energize the body, strengthening the back and all the muscles that support it. These poses also expand the heart area, helping yogis become more open to the world.

Cobra  Bhujangasana

In this graceful pose, you emulate the elegant cobra as it lifts its upper body and spreads open the hood on its head.

Benefits
- Develops flexibility in the upper spine.
- Stretches and strengthens the muscles of the back and neck.
- Stretches and tones the abdominal organs.
- Opens up the chest.

When to Be Careful
- If your back is weak, be especially aware of using your back muscles and not your hands.
- If you feel stress in your lower back, open your legs a bit.

1 Lie on your belly in Corpse pose (page 38).

2 Bring your legs and feet together. Place your palms on the floor with your fingertips under your shoulders. Your elbows should be pointing toward the ceiling and your arms should be close to your body.

3 Place your forehead on the floor.

4 On an inhalation, use your back muscles to gently lift your upper body forward as your raise your head, neck, and chest off the floor. Keep your legs and feet together.

5 Roll your shoulders back and down away from your ears. This will cause your neck to feel longer and your chest to open up. Remember not to put pressure on your hands and be careful not to scrunch up the back of your neck.

6 Concentrate on your upper spine. Breathe slowly and with control.

7 To come out of the pose, exhale and gently release one vertebrae at a time, lowering first your chest, then your chin, and finally your forehead to the floor.

8 If you'd like to do a second round, first turn your cheek to the opposite side and rest a moment, keeping your arms and legs in place.

9 Rest in Corpse on your belly.

Locust Salabasana

Locusts aren't the most lovable insects, but yogis are very fond of this pose! It helps to develop a sense of determination and strength of will.

Benefits

- Strengthens the lower back, pelvis, and abdomen.
- Increases flexibility in the lower back.
- Relieves constipation.

Tips from the yogis

- The closer you are able to bring your arms together, the better massage your belly gets.

- If your breasts are on the big side, use your arms to press them together and slightly upward.

- If you're having difficulty getting your arms under your body, just place them alongside your body with your palms on the floor.

- As you prepare to go into the pose, tuck your toes under and push your body forward so more weight rests on your shoulders. Then, release the tops of your feet back to the floor.

- If your legs shake, you've come up too high. Lower them a bit to reduce the strain.

- You can warm up for Locust by doing a Half Locust. Raise your right leg, then lower it, and then raise your left leg.

1 Starting from Corpse on your belly, bring your arms under your body by gently rocking from side to side. Face your palms up so your thighs rest on them. Bring your chin to the floor.

2 On an inhalation reach your legs back to the wall behind you and raise them up off the floor slowly and with control.

3 Keep your legs straight and focus on elongating your lower back.

4 Bring your legs up only as high as you can maintain a steady, comfortable posture. Height is not the most important thing! Remember to keep your chin on the floor.

5 To come out of the pose, exhale as you gently lower your legs to the floor.

6 Before doing a second round, rest on your belly in step 1 (Corpse pose) for a few minutes with your cheek to one side.

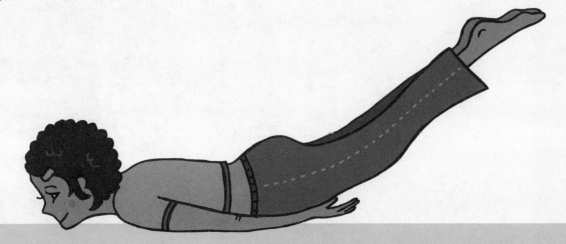

Bow ✿ Dhanurasana

Bow is a good pose to do when you only have time for one backward bend.

Benefits

- Intensifies all the benefits of Cobra and Locust.
- Extends and strengthens the entire spine.
- Regulates your periods.
- Releases stiffness in the shoulders.

When to Be Careful

Avoid doing this pose if you have high blood pressure.

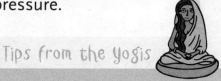

Tips from the Yogis

- If you do a second round, try lifting your upper body first and then your lower body.
- For a great massage to the belly, get comfortable in the position, deepen your breathing, and allow the breath to rock you back and forth.
- When preparing to go into the pose, or between rounds, massage the arches of your feet. It will feel great and you'll be massaging the pressure points that correspond to the organs being massaged in the pose.
- As you become more comfortable with the pose, you can try bringing your feet, knees, and thighs close together.
- Avoid holding your toes. Your feet might cramp.

1 Begin in Corpse on your belly. Bend your knees and bring your heels toward your buttocks. Reach your arms back and take hold of your feet, ankles, or shins. Your knees and feet can be as close together (or as far part) as comfortable.

2 Rest your forehead on the floor.

3 With your arms straight, begin to press your legs into your hands.

4 As you inhale, use your arms like a bowstring and raise the lower half of your body off the floor.

5 Stretch your head, neck, and chest forward as you raise them off the floor. Balance on your belly and be careful not to scrunch your neck.

6 Keep your arms strong while you expand your chest and relax the muscles along your spine. Concentrate on your entire spine.

7 When you're ready to come out of the pose, exhale and lower your legs, then your chest, then chin and forehead to the floor.

8 If you're going to do a second round, you can keep hold of your legs, allowing your feet to flop out to the side and turn your cheek to the side.

9 Bow is pretty intense. Take a rest in Corpse pose if you need to.

In yoga, resting is as important as movement. As with any sport or strenuous activity, if you don't take a breather, you will soon become exhausted.

Resting between poses is good for you in so many ways. While resting, your body is better able to absorb the many benefits of each pose. Resting rejuvenates, giving you a boost of energy to practice the next series of poses. And by easing muscle tension and calming the mind, you can prevent injury and strain.

Use these poses to rest between asanas, or whenever you need to recharge.

Corpse  Savasana and Advasana

Corpse is the ideal relaxation pose for yoga. When you rest in Corpse, you release all the tension in your mind and body. Experiment with a pillow under your knees or head to make sure your body is completely relaxed.

1 For *Savasana*, lie on your back with your arms slightly away from your sides, palms up and legs spread comfortably apart.

2 Breathe slowly and naturally. Send a mental message of relaxation to any areas of tension. When you're ready to move, come out slowly and gently.

3 Corpse on your belly is called *Advasana*. Put your arms alongside your body, palms facing up, legs comfortably apart, and cheek to one side.

Child's Pose
Balasana

Child's pose helps stretch out the back. It's a wonderful pose to rest in after the backward bending poses, as well as arm strengtheners like Downward Facing Dog.

1 Starting in Corpse on your belly, bring your legs together and place the palms of your hands on the floor beside your chest.

2 Use your hands to push your hips back and rest your buttocks on your heels.

3 Place your forehead on the floor, bring your arms alongside your legs (with palms facing up), and let your shoulders droop forward.

4 Relax in this pose for as long as you like. Feel the stretch in your lower back as your thighs massage your belly and pelvis.

5 Try placing a pillow underneath your forehead if your head hurts.

6 For an additional stretch, reach your arms out in front of you along the floor, extending your upper body forward.

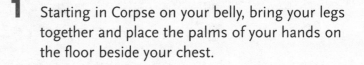

Backward Bends energize the body by building up heat, but Forward Bends cool things down. They release physical, mental, and emotional strain, increase patience, and ease anxiety. It's very easy for the mind to wander when you're in a Forward Bend. If your mind is busy elsewhere, try bringing your focus gently back to your breathing.

Head to Knee Pose
✿ Janusirshasana ✿

Like all Forward Bends, Head to Knee pose is great for stretching the hamstrings and lower spine. And as with all the yoga poses, there are many cool benefits for the body that we can't even see!

Benefits

- Helps with digestion.
- Stretches the muscles between the ribs.
- Massages the liver and tones the kidneys.

1 Sit on the floor and stretch your legs straight in front of you, toes pointing up toward the ceiling.

2 Bend your left knee and bring the sole of your left foot as far up along the inside of your right leg as is comfortable. Open your left knee to rest on the floor.

3 Keep your hips even (in other words, don't lean to one side and don't keep one hip further forward than the other). Check to make sure your back is nice and straight.

4 Inhale, stretching your arms straight up overhead alongside your ears. Keep your shoulders relaxed and down away from your ears.

5 As you exhale, bend forward from the hips, keeping your back straight for as long as possible and your upper body toward the wall in front of you.

6 Maintaining the forward stretch, release your body over your right leg. Relax your head, neck, and chest.

7 Let your arms rest anywhere along the right leg that is comfortable—the foot, ankle, or shin—without using your hands to pull you further down.

8 Keep extending out from your lower back. This will help lengthen your stretch.

9 To come out of the pose, stretch your arms out in front of you, inhale, and come into an upright position with your back as flat as possible.

10 Release your arms and legs, then shake them out a bit. Reverse the leg position and repeat on the other side.

Tips from the Yogis

- If you find that your back is rounded when seated, place a cushion or towel just under your buttocks to help straighten your back.
- If you're flexible and your hands reach comfortably to your toes, you can wrap your fingers around your big toes and place your thumbs on the top of the big toes.

🌸 Full Forward Bend 🌸
Paschimotanasana

The Full Forward Bend pose actually has several long Sanskrit names. *Paschimotanasana* indicates the stretching of the entire back of the body. There is also *Ugrasana*, meaning "formidable" and *Brahmacharyasana*, meaning "self-restraint." (Try saying those names three times fast!) No matter how you say it, the benefits of this forward bending pose are great!

Benefits

- Tones the stomach.
- Improves digestion.
- Relieves wind.
- Energizes the entire spine.
- Massages the heart.

1 Sit on the floor with your legs together and stretched straight out in front of you. Your toes should be pointing up toward the ceiling.

2 Use your hands to move the flesh from underneath your buttocks so your sitz bones (buttocks bones) are flat on the floor or cushion.

3 Straighten your back, inhale, and bring your arms straight up alongside your ears.

4 As you exhale, bend forward from your hips. Keep your back straight for as long as comfortable, stretching your upper body forward. In your mind's eye, visualize your upper body lying flat against your thighs.

5 Relax your head, neck, and chest so they hang comfortably.

6 Take hold of your legs wherever it's comfortable—shins, ankles, or toes—or rest your hands alongside your legs. Keep your shoulders back and relaxed, not shrugged.

7 Focus on gently stretching your lower back and hamstrings.

8 If you're really flexible, try wrapping your fingers around your feet, and place your thumbs on top of your big toes.

9 When you're ready to come out of the pose, reach your arms out in front of you and stretch back up into an upright position.

10 Release your arms and legs, then shake them out.

Think of a soaking wet sponge. To be able to use it without dripping water, you need to twist it several times and wring out the water. That's what Twists do for yogis. They literally help wring out everyday toxins that can accumulate in your digestive system. That's why Twists are great poses to finish up a yoga session.

Half Spinal Twist Ardha Matsyendrasana

Half Spinal Twist can be tough to do because getting into the pose can sometimes be confusing. That may be why the ancient texts say that it helps increase a yogi's determination!

Benefits

- Helps make your spine more flexible.
- Stretches your buttocks.
- Opens up your chest.
- May relieve hay fever or bronchitis!

When to Be Careful

- If you have a slipped disk or lower back problems, use extreme caution.

1 Sit on the floor with your legs straight in front of you. Keep your back straight and your belly relaxed.

2 Bending your right knee, place your right foot on the floor on the outside of the left leg close to the knee. Take hold of your right knee. Sit tall, stretching your back upward.

3 On an exhalation, twist your upper body to the right and place your right palm on the floor as close to the base of your spine as possible. This hand will help to keep your back straight.

4 Bring your left arm between your bent knee and your chest, bending your elbow so your hand reaches up and your elbow gently pushes against the outside of your upraised knee.

5 Keep stretching your back upward as you gently twist a little further to the right, looking over your right shoulder. Check to see that one shoulder is not higher than the other. Your belly muscles and legs should be relaxed. Be sure to sit up straight.

6 To come out of the pose, inhale and leading with the head exhale as you twist back to face center. Releasing your arms, twist around slightly to the left for a little extra stretch.

7 Release your legs and shake them out before reversing the leg position and twisting to the other side.

Tips from the yogis

- If it's difficult to keep your back straight while your legs are still in front of you, put a small pillow or cushion under your buttocks.
- If it's difficult keeping your back straight in the bent leg position, reposition your foot.

You've stretched your spine, massaged your belly, expanded your chest, released tension in your shoulders, and lots more. Now it's time to lock in all the good things, so they can stay with you and help you throughout the entire day.

✼ Yogic Seal ✼ Yoga Mudra

In Sanskrit, *Yoga Mudra* means "to draw forth the pleasure of yoga." That is why it's such a wonderful pose to practice at the end of a session.

Benefits
- Tones the nervous system.
- Relieves problems in the belly.

1 Sit in a comfortable cross-legged position on the floor.

2 Check your posture to make sure your back is straight, your belly is relaxed, and your shoulders are back.

3 Bring your arms behind your back and take hold of either wrist with the opposite hand.

4 Inhale, and as you exhale, gently fold forward from your hips, lengthening your spine until your forehead rests on the floor.

5 With your hands still behind you, relax your head, neck, and shoulders.

6 Focus on your breathing and relax.

7 When you're ready to come out of the pose, inhale as you slowly raise your head and stretch your body forward, and come back to a seated position.

8 Gently place your hands on your lap or knees and relax.

Tips from the yogis

- Don't worry if your forehead doesn't reach the floor. Just relax in the pose wherever it's comfortable.
- If your buttocks come up when your head touches the floor, try putting a pillow or cushion under your forehead.
- If you like, you can bring the tips of your index finger and thumb together to make an OK sign. This is the hand position called *Chin Mudra* and symbolizes the joining of You (the index finger) with the Universe (the thumb).

Yogic sleep is a very important part of your total yoga practice. It helps you cool down after all the warming up you just did in the previous poses. Don't be surprised if you feel a little cold. It is a good idea to put on socks and a sweater, or put a blanket over you to make sure you stay warm.

You should begin by having the room dark, but not so dark that you can't see. You can put a towel or pillow under your knees to help keep your back flat on the floor. You can also use a small pillow under your head if your neck feels sore. The key is to be comfy!

❀ Yogic Sleep ❀ Yoga Nidra

Resting and allowing your body to reap the benefits of all the asanas is just as important as breathing. When you're in Yogic Sleep, your body should be completely relaxed and your mind should be calm but awake.

Benefits
- Absorbs all the positive results of the poses.
- Reduces stress.
- Calms your mind.

1 Lay on your back in Corpse pose.

2 Inhale deeply and tense each and every muscle of your entire body.

3 Raise your arms, legs, back, and head about an inch off the floor while you balance on your buttocks. Make a prune face scrunching all the facial muscles up toward the nose. Inhale deeply. Open your mouth, and let all the air out as you release your body to the floor.

4 Repeat steps two and three, this time opening your mouth wide and sticking your tongue way out to reach your chin while your eyes look up to your forehead. Inhale deeply. Exhale, roaring like a lioness as you release your body to the floor.

5 Rock your arms and legs gently, and then let them rest.

6 Rock your head gently from side to side, and then let it rest.

7 If there are still areas that feel tense, send a mental message of relaxation to that area. You are a yogi! Your mind has that power.

8 Rest for about five minutes (or longer if you like), remaining perfectly still as you simply observe your breathing and thoughts. Try to keep your mind awake, but don't sweat it if you fall asleep.

9 When you're ready to "wake up:"

- Slowly start to wiggle your toes and fingers, then rock your arms and legs gently.
- Stretch your body as if you were just waking up from a good night's sleep.
- Lay on your right side for a few moments, with your head resting on your right arm and your knees drawn up toward your chest.
- Slowly sit up into a comfortable position. Take a moment to enjoy how rested and alert you feel.

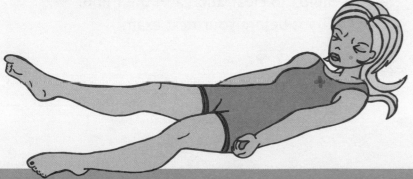

Professional athletes, dancers, singers, and even actors all say that good breathing practices are an important part of their success. In yoga, it's especially important! In Sanskrit, *prana* means "breath" or "life force." It is the energy that flows throughout your body and even the universe. *Yama* means "mastery." When you learn to control your breathing, the poses become easier and you have better control in your practice. Yoga teaches many different breathing techniques, each intended to help the mind and body in different ways.

Deep Breathing Deergha Swaasam

Sometimes called three-part breathing, this practice is a wonderful way to maximize your lung capacity because you can take in as much as seven times the normal amount of air you breathe! Deep Breathing helps get rid of tension and strengthens your lungs. It can even help cure hiccups!

Benefits

- Energizes your entire system.
- Helps to clear and calm the mind. (Try it before your next exam!)

1 Check your posture.

2 Inhale through your nose slowly and deeply, feeling your belly expand, then your chest, and finally your collarbones.

3 Exhale through your nose slowly and with control. Feel your collarbones release and then your chest. Gently tuck in your abdomen to push out as much air possible.

4 Repeat, continuing in this way for a few minutes. See if you can keep your inhalations and exhalations equal. (So if it takes three counts to inhale, take three counts to exhale.)

5 When you're ready to stop, return your breathing to normal after an exhalation.

Tips from the yogis

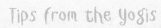

- When you're doing the breathing practices, you want to be comfortable and relaxed with your back straight and your chest open.
- If sitting or kneeling on the floor is uncomfortable, sit in a straight-backed chair with your feet firmly on the ground.
- Rest your hands on your lap or knees.

Alternate Nostril Breathing
Nadi Suddhi

The Sanskrit name, *Nadi Suddhi*, actually means "nerve purification." And that is exactly what this exercise does for your nervous system! It is one of the most important and powerful of the breathing practices.

Benefits
- Balances the two sides of your brain.
- Helps to focus the mind.
- Great preparation for meditation.

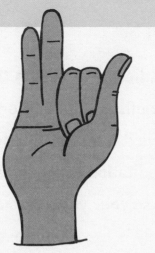

1 Check your posture. Make sure your belly is relaxed.

2 Make a gentle fist with your right hand. Release your thumb, ring, and pinky fingers. This is called *Vishnu Mudra* and is intended to help with relaxation.

3 Close off your right nostril with your thumb. Exhale slowly through your left nostril.

4 Inhale slowly through the left nostril.

5 Close off your left nostril with the ring and pinky fingers of your right hand. At the same time release your thumb from your right nostril, and exhale slowly.

6 Continue at your own pace, keeping the breath relaxed and quiet.

7 When you are ready to stop, your last exhalation should be through your right nostril for balance.

8 Return your hand to your lap (or knee) and your breath to normal.

Tips from the yogis

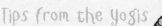
- Over time, try to make your exhalations twice as long as your inhalations. So if it takes three counts to inhale, use six counts to exhale.

Meditation

Meditation focuses and clears the mind, creating a state of tranquility, concentration, and peace. Various forms of meditation have been practiced around the world since people started thinking about the universe around them.

Some people meditate to help them become closer to the Divine. In fact, prayer can be considered a form of meditation. Others practice because it helps them maintain a clear head as they go about their daily activities. But no matter why (or even how) you meditate, scientific studies have shown that the benefits of meditation are great. Give it a try and see for yourself! Meditation is a wonderful way to close your yoga sessions. Your body is fresh and rested and your mind is clear and focused. However, you can meditate any time that feels right for you. Many people like to practice meditation first thing in the morning to help prepare for the day. Others practice to inspire calm after a hectic day at school or work. Still others find meditating before bedtime helps them sleep better.

Types of Meditation

No matter what form of meditation you practice, there is one thing you can count on—your mind will wander. That is its nature. When you realize your mind has drifted off elsewhere, gently (and without frustration or scolding) bring it back to your focal point.

MANTRA (JAPA)   Repeating a short uplifting phrase (either silently or aloud) helps quiet the mind by allowing it to focus on only one thing. A common practice is to repeat the mystical word "Om." You might choose to repeat an affirmation like, "I am happy and at peace." Or you can choose a short passage from the *Bible* or other spiritual text.

FOCUSING ON THE BREATH   Simply focusing on the breath, without altering or forcing it, is another way to calm and still the mind.

MINDFULNESS (VIPASSANA)   In this practice, the yogi simply observes her thoughts as they pass in and out of her mind. She does not judge them or even examine them, allowing them to float by like clouds on a breezy day.

VISUALIZATION   In your mind's eye, visualize something that makes you feel calm and peaceful. It could be your image of the Divine, a beautiful flower, a place that makes you happy, or anything that brings you a sense of peace.

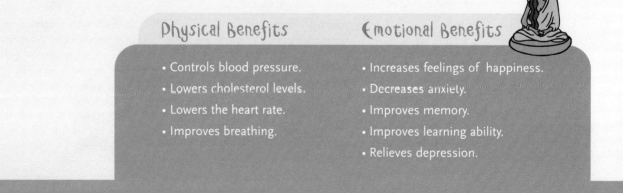

Physical Benefits

- Controls blood pressure.
- Lowers cholesterol levels.
- Lowers the heart rate.
- Improves breathing.

Emotional Benefits

- Increases feelings of happiness.
- Decreases anxiety.
- Improves memory.
- Improves learning ability.
- Relieves depression.

Preparing for Meditation:

1 It's best to have a set time and place that fits in easily with your schedule. This is the surest way to practice regularly and reap the maximum benefits.

2 Choose a quiet place where you can practice for as long as you want without being distracted or interrupted.

3 Make a commitment to practice for a specific length of time and stick to it. You can start with as little as three minutes and gradually increase the time to as much as 30 minutes—or even more!

4 Always try to meditate on an empty stomach.

5 Just as there are many ways to practice Hatha, there are many ways to meditate. (Some yogis even think of their Hatha practice as a moving meditation.) Experiment until you find one that you like.

Postures for Meditation

How you sit is important. You want your back to be straight and your body to be at ease so you won't be tempted to fidget. Here are some different poses to try. Experiment with leg positioning and other ways to get comfortable in each pose.

Comfortable Pose
❀ Sukhasana ❀

Simply sit with your legs crossed in front of you under your thighs. You can have one leg resting on the other, or have both legs resting on the ground with your ankles aligned.

Lotus Pose Padmasana

This is the pose everyone thinks they have to do to be a good yogi. (But you don't.) It's very challenging for many people, and is especially hard on your knees.

1 Gently bring the foot of one leg to rest on the opposite thigh.

2 Fold the other leg so its heel rests under the opposite thigh. This is Half Lotus pose (*Ardha Padmasana*).

3 If you want to move into the full position, bring the lower foot up so it rests on the thigh of your upper leg.

Hero Pose
Vajrasana

Sit on your knees with your buttocks resting on your heels. Your hands should rest comfortably on your lap or knees.

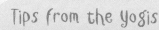

Tips from the Yogis

- If your back curves, place a pillow under your buttocks to help bring your hips above your knees.

- If your knees don't touch the floor (or if they feel strained), try putting a pillow under them as well.

Now, you've learned some of yoga's fundamental poses. Take the time you need to master them, trying some of the suggestions offered, and exploring ways they work best for you.

There are so many poses to choose from—enough so that you can make each practice session different from the last! And as your skills increase, you can start mixing it up even more by adding additional poses to your workout for continued variety.

Cat and Cow

Some yogis like to stretch a little at the very beginning of practice or before they begin Sun Salutation by practicing a pose like Cat and Cow.

Benefits
- Loosens your back.
- Opens your hips.
- Energizes your spine.

Cat

1 Get onto your hands and knees. Place your palms directly under your shoulders and your knees directly under your hips.

2 Exhale slowly, tuck your tailbone under, bring your chin toward your chest, and arch your back high in the air. Imagine you are a cat stretching after a nap.

3 As you inhale, release your belly toward the floor, lift your tailbone, and extend out through your chin. Now you look like a cow!

4 Practice for as long as is comfortable, breathing slowly and deeply and using the breath to shift from Cat to Cow. You might even want to exaggerate the stretch a bit.

5 When you're ready to stop, come back to step 1. From here you can either push back into Child's pose, or tuck your toes under and push up into Downward Dog.

Tips from the yogis

- If your wrists are sore or a bit weak, try making fists. Then, extend your thumbs, and place your knuckles on the floor. Or, you can bend your arms and place your forearms on the floor.

Cow

Triangle ❀ Trikonasana

When you are in this pose, you create triangles with your legs and arms. This is a great pose to ease your period cramps. But it has lots of other benefits as well!

Benefits

- Opens up your hips and chest.
- Stretches the muscles surrounding the rib cage.
- Strengthens your neck.

1 Spread your legs about 4–4 1/2 feet apart, open your right foot out to a 90° angle, and bring your left foot inward to a 45° angle. Check to see that your hips are squared center. (This is the same opening stance as Warrior II).

2 Inhale as you move your arms up so they are parallel to the floor. Tighten your right thigh muscles.

3 Exhaling, shift your pelvis to the left, while you extend your upper body out and over the right leg, bending at the waist. Your right arm should reach down toward the floor behind your right leg and your left arm should reach up toward the ceiling. Expand your chest. Your legs should be straight and the whole of your left foot should stay firmly on the floor.

4 If the fingertips of your lower hand touch the floor, great. If not, your hand can rest gently on your front leg, either on the thigh, shin, or you can even use a small stool or chair.

5 Check that the weight of your body is evenly distributed between both legs.

6 Turn your head and look up at your left hand.

7 When you are ready to come out of the pose, stretch back up to center as you inhale. Reverse the leg and arm positions and practice on the other side.

Eagle  Garudasana

Eagle pose is one of the most challenging balancing poses. You really have to concentrate to be able to wrap your arms and legs in so many different directions!

Benefits

- Opens up the hips, thighs, and ankles.
- Expands the upper back and shoulders.
- Creates a sense of being strong and grounded.

Tips from the Yogis

- It's OK if your palms don't come together. You can either have the fingers of the lower hand resting in your upper palm, or clasp the thumb of your upper hand.
- If your foot doesn't wrap fully around your calf, bring it around as far as is comfortable. With practice, it will.
- Balance can be tough in this pose. You can let the toes of the leg that wraps around rest gently on the floor.

1 Choose a fixed point on the wall in front of you.

2 Starting in Mountain pose, bend your right elbow and bring it up in front of your chest. Keep your upper arm parallel to the floor.

3 Wrap your left arm under, up, and around the right, working to bring your hands together with the palms as close as possible.

4 Raise your elbows so they become level with your shoulders. Your forearms and fingers should reach up toward the ceiling. Your shoulders will come forward a bit, opening up the shoulder blades.

5 Raise your right leg and balance on your left. Bend your right knee, bring your right leg over the left so the right thigh rests on top of the left.

6 Wrap your right foot back behind the calf of your left leg.

7 Keep your legs bent and stretch your upper body toward the ceiling. Check to see that your hips are even.

8 When you're ready to come out of the pose, slowly unwrap your arms and legs and come back into Mountain.

9 Reverse the arm and leg positions and practice on the other side.

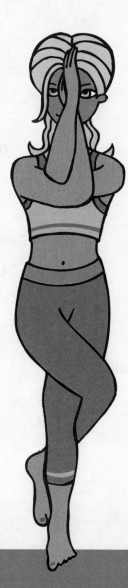

❁ Backward Boat Pose ❁
Poorna Nauasana

In Backward Boat pose, you enhance many of the benefits achieved in Cobra and Locust.

Benefits

- Strengthens and stretches the spine.
- Gives a nice massage to the belly.
- Helps with indigestion.

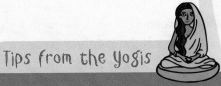

Tips from the yogis

- It can be challenging to keep your legs together. It's OK to open your legs up to hip-width apart.

- Some yogis like to bend their knees to ease any strain on their lower backs.

- This is a challenging pose. If you're feeling any strain simply come out of it—slowly and with control.

1 Lie on your belly. Place your legs together and your forehead on the floor. Stretch your arms straight ahead, alongside your ears.

2 Interlock your thumbs, keep your arms alongside your ears, and inhale as you raise both the lower and upper half of your body up off the floor. Balance on your stomach.

3 When you're ready to come out of the pose, exhale as you lower your arms and legs.

4 Rest in Corpse on your belly.

✿ Forward Boat Pose ✿
Paschima Nauasana

Forward Boat pose is a balancing pose as well as a forward bend.

Benefits

- Strengthens the belly muscles and hips.
- Tones the belly organs (including the liver, gall bladder, and kidneys).
- Improves digestion.

Tips from the yogis

- Be aware of your back. It should be straight and at about a 45° angle from the floor.
- Remember to balance on your buttocks.
- As you get stronger in the pose, try starting from Corpse pose, raising first your legs, then your upper body.

1 Sit on the floor with your legs stretched out in front of you and your palms on the floor near your buttocks. Check to make sure your back is nice and straight.

2 Keep your legs straight and your weight on the back of your buttocks. Exhale and raise your legs up off the floor so your feet are about shoulder height.

3 Raise your arms so they are parallel to the floor. Balance only on your buttocks.

4 Breathe easily and hold the pose for as long as is comfortable. Come down on an exhalation.

Revolved Triangle  Parivitta  Trikonasana

**This pose is helpful for
easing backaches. It can also become
a part of your regular yoga routine.**

1 Come into the same starting stance as in regular Triangle, with your right foot open.

2 Twist around to the right with your hands on your hips.

3 Exhale and extend through your spine. Lower your upper body as far as is comfortable over your right leg. Your legs should stay strong and straight and your weight should be evenly distributed between both legs.

4 Twist to the right and bring the fingertips of your left hand to the outside of your right foot. Reach your right hand high into the sky, opening up your chest. Look up toward your right hand.

5 To come out of this pose, inhale as you reverse the twist, raise your upper body, and turn to center. Reverse your stance and practice on the other side.

Tips from the yogis

- If you feel unbalanced with your hand on the outside of your foot, place it alongside the inside.
- If your fingertips won't reach the floor, you can use a pillow, folded blanket, or stool to rest on.

Bent Hero Pose Supta Vajrasana

Bent Hero pose will calm you and can ease discomfort in your pelvis.

1 Fold a blanket a few times so it's long and thick like a log. (You'll want to experiment with the thickness that works best for you.)

2 Sit in Hero pose. Place the short end of the blanket behind you, about six inches away from your buttocks.

3 Using your arms for support, bend backward, resting your entire back and head on the blanket. Raise your arms overhead and bring them to rest on the floor behind you.

4 Stay in this position for about five minutes. Use your arms to come back up. If your knees are uncomfortable, try sitting in Lotus or Easy pose.

✾ Lying Knee ✾ to Chest Twist

This is a good pose to ease cramps and backache.

1 From Corpse, spread your arms along the floor into a "T." Inhale, bend your knees, and bring them up to your chest.

2 Keeping your shoulders firmly on the floor, exhale as you twist to the right, bringing your knees to the floor. Look over your left shoulder.

3 To come out of the pose, inhale as you twist your head and knees back to center.

4 Rest a moment and practice on the other side.

Glossary

Affirmation: A positive thought or statement.

Ahimsa (Ah-HIM-sah): A Sanskrit word meaning "causing no pain." Commonly used to mean non-violence in word and deed.

Asanas (A-sah-naz): Poses. Sanskrit word meaning "steady, comfortable pose."

Ashtanga (ash-TANG-a): A Sanskrit word meaning eight-limbed and indicating Patanjali's eight stages of yoga. Also known as Raja Yoga, an aerobic style of Hatha yoga practice.

Bhakti (Bahk-tee) yoga: The path of yoga that emphasizes devotion.

Bikram yoga: A style of yoga developed by Bikram Choudry that is practiced in a warm, humid room.

Chi (Qi): Like prana, the Asian concept of life force.

Chin mudra (chin MOO-dra): A mudra whereby the thumb and index finger join to symbolize the bowing of the individual consciousness to the supreme consciousness.

Guru (GU-ru): Sanskrit for spiritual teacher.

Hatha (HA-tha): A Sanskrit word combining *ha* "sun" and *tha* "moon." The physical practice of yoga including poses, breathing, and relaxation.

Integral yoga: A style of yoga that combines the various paths to enable integration into everyday life. Developed by Swami Satchidananda.

Iyengar (EYE-yen-gar) yoga: A style of Hatha yoga that emphasizes detailed placement of the body. Developed by B.K.S. Iyengar.

Japa (JA-pa) yoga: The path of yoga that emphasizes repetition of a mantra.

Jnana (YAN-a) yoga: The path of yoga that emphasizes wisdom.

Karma (KAR-ma) yoga: The path of yoga that emphasizes service through action.

Kundalini (kun-da-LEE-nee): The energy residing in the base of the spine. A style of Hatha yoga, combining breathing, poses, chanting, and meditation to awaken and release the Kundalini energy.

Mantra (MAN-tra): A sound, word, or string of words that when chanted aloud or silently helps focus the mind in meditation.

Meditation: The practice of focusing the mind to achieve inner peace and stillness.

Mudra (MOO-dra): A Sanskrit word meaning "to draw pleasure from." A series of positions, generally for the hands, that enhances the Hatha practice.

Namaste (NAH-ma-stay): A Sanskrit word meaning "the divine in me honors the divine in you." A traditional Hindu greeting accompanied by a short bow with the hands together in front of the head or chest.

Om: Cosmic sound vibration that contains all the sounds of the universe.

Patanjali (pa-TAN-ja-li): Often considered the father of yoga, organized the entire yoga practice into *The Yoga Sutras*.

Prana (PRAH-na): A Sanskrit word meaning "breath" or "life force."

Pranayama (prah-na-YAH-ma): A Sanskrit word meaning "mastery of breath or life force." Also refers to the breathing practices.

Raja (RA-ja) yoga: The path of yoga that emphasizes control of the mind through concentration and meditation.

Sage: A wise person.

Samadhi (sa-MAH-di): The highest state of meditation; the super-conscious state.

Sanskrit (SAN-skrit): The ancient Indian language used in yoga.

Sutra (SU-tra): A Sanskrit word meaning "thread." Short sayings that impart an important spiritual truth.

Swami: A spiritually wise individual. A monk.

Vinyasa (vin-YA-sa): A style of yoga where poses flow from one to the other.

Vipassana (vi-PAH-sana): A meditation practice involving observation of one's thoughts.

Yama (YA-ma): A Sanskrit word meaning mastery.

Yoga: A Sanskrit word meaning "union." The world's oldest ongoing personal development system for mind, body, and spirit.

Yogi: A person who practices yoga.

Index

Credits

Jeanne Finestone, Author
It was love at first asana for Jeanne "Chandrika" Finestone. A yoga practitioner for over 15 years, Jeanne teaches at the Integral Yoga Institute in New York City. She has held senior level positions in the publishing and television industries, and is now enjoying a career as a freelance writer and independent producer.

Shelly Meridith Delice, Illustrator
Shelly Meridith Delice grew up in a small farm town in Kansas. She now lives in a loft in New York City with her husband and daughter, Zinedine. She has been designing toys and illustrating books for 15 years.